(Eileen 4th Sept 2011)

THIS BOOK

Belongs to Christine

My Friend.

Have A Blessed

70th Birthday.

"Poem" Pg 65

Christine

love

Eileen x

A Book
of Prayers

TO KEEP FOR EVER

Compiled by Sophie Piper
Illustrated by Ian Mitchell

LION

Written and compiled by Sophie Piper
Illustrations copyright © 2002 Ian Mitchell
This edition copyright © 2002 Lion Hudson

A Lion Book
an imprint of
Lion Hudson plc
Wilkinson House, Jordan Hill Road,
Oxford OX2 8DR, England
www.lionhudson.com
ISBN 978-0-7459-4755-6 (white gift edition)
ISBN 978-0-7459-4827-0 (blue gift edition)

First edition 2002
10 9 8

Acknowledgments
All prayers that have not been credited are by Sophie Piper,
copyright © Lion Hudson. Prayers by Lois Rock on
pp. 9, 21, 33, 56, 66, 71, 79, 82 are copyright © Lion Hudson.

A catalogue record for this book is available
from the British Library

Typeset in 15/18 Venetian 301 BT
Printed and bound in China

Contents

Introduction

Prayer is spending time with God.

It can be a time for talking: talking to God about your hopes and dreams, your fears and worries; about things you want to celebrate and things you are sorry about.

It can be a time for sitting quietly, trusting that God will speak to you in your thoughts, helping you to understand more about God and more about yourself.

In these ways, prayer can help guide you to learn from the past to live wisely in the future... to live in the way that is good and right, with God as a companion and a friend.

May this collection of prayers that other people have said help you in your prayers.

Learning to Pray

Here I am
beneath the sky
and all alone
in prayer;
but I know
God is listening,
for God is everywhere.

Lois Rock

Come into my soul, Lord,
as the dawn breaks into the sky;
let your sun rise in my heart
at the coming of the day.

Traditional

In the rush and noise of life, as you have intervals, step within yourselves and be still. Wait upon God and feel his good presence; this will carry you through your day's business.

William Penn (1644–1718)

God be in my head,
  And in my understanding;
God be in mine eyes,
  And in my looking;
God be in my mouth,
  And in my speaking;
God be in my heart,
  And in my thinking;
God be at my end,
  And at my departing.

Sarum primer (1527)

Lord, you know what I want.
If you think it right, may I have it.
If you do not think it right,
good Lord, do not be displeased
    that I asked,
for I don't want anything that you
    don't want.

After Julian of Norwich (1342–c. 1416)

God help my thoughts! they stray from me, setting off on the wildest journeys; when I am at prayer, they run off like naughty children, making trouble. When I read the Bible, they fly to a distant place, filled with seductions. My thoughts can cross an ocean with a single leap; they can fly from earth to heaven, and back again, in a single second. They come to me for a fleeting moment, and then away they flee. No chains, no locks can hold them back; no threats of punishment can restrain them, no hiss of a lash can frighten them. They slip from my grasp like tails of eels, they swoop hither and thither like swallows in flight.

Dear, chaste Christ, who can see into every heart, and read every mind, take hold of my thoughts. Bring my thoughts back to me, and clasp me to yourself.

Author unknown

O make my heart so still, so still,
When I am deep in prayer,
That I might hear the white mist-wreaths
Losing themselves in air!

Utsonomya San, Japan

There is no place where God is not,
wherever I go, there God is.
Now and always he upholds me with
   his power
and keeps me safe in his love.

Author unknown

Faith in God

All things praise thee Lord most high!
Heaven and earth and sea and sky!

Time and space are praising thee!
All things praise thee; Lord, may we!

George William Condor (1821–74)

Our God is the God of all,
The God of heaven and earth,
Of the sea and the rivers;
The God of the sun and of the moon
    and of all the stars;
The God of the lofty mountains
    and of the lowly valleys,
He has His dwelling around heaven
    and earth, and sea, and all that in
    them is.

St Patrick (389–461)

White are the wavetops,
White is the snow:
Great is the One
Who made all things below.

Green are the grasslands,
Green is the tree:
Great is the One
Who has made you and me.

Blue are the cornflowers,
Blue is the sky:
Great is the One
Who made all things on high.

Gold is the harvest,
Gold is the sun:
God is our Maker –
Great is the One.

Lois Rock

Kind Jesus

Shelter me
from the storms that alarm me.

Shepherd me
and in safety enfold me.

Shine your light
on the path that you show me.

Lord Jesus, you are my light
In the darkness,
You are my warmth
In the cold,
You are my happiness
In sorrow…

Author unknown

We celebrate the birth of Jesus:
for God has come among us.

We celebrate the birth of Jesus:
for heaven has come to earth.

We celebrate the birth of Jesus:
and let love grow between us.

We celebrate the birth of Jesus:
and live as God's children on earth.

Blessed be the name of Jesus, who
  died to save us.
Blessed be Jesus, who had compassion
  on us.
Blessed be Jesus, who suffered
  loneliness, rejection and pain, for
  our sakes.
Blessed be Jesus, through whose cross
  I am forgiven.
Lord Jesus, deepen my understanding
  of your suffering and death.

Written by young people in Kenya

Thank You

Thank you, dear God,
for the joy of life
and the everyday things
that make life a joy.

My Father, for another night
Of quiet sleep and rest,
For all the joy of morning light,
Your holy name be blest.

Henry William Baker (1821–77)

For this new morning and its light,
For rest and shelter of the night,
For health and food, for love and friends,
For every gift your goodness sends,
We thank you, gracious Lord.

Author unknown

For food in a world where many walk
    in hunger;
For faith in a world where many walk
    in fear;
For friends in a world where many walk
    alone,
We give you humble thanks, O Lord.

A Girl Guide world hunger grace

Each time we eat,
May we remember God's love.

Chinese grace

For health and strength and daily food,
we praise your name, O Lord.

Traditional

Dear God,
Thank you for the things I have in
    abundance,
to enjoy with frivolity.

Thank you for the things of which
    I have enough,
to enjoy thoughtfully.

Thank you for the things that I lack
that keep me trusting in your many
blessings.

Thank you, dear God,
for the blessing of things that stay
    the same:
for people we have known for ever
and the familiar paths where we walk.

Thank you, dear God,
for the blessing of things that change:
for newcomers with their new customs,
new ways of doing things, new paths
    to discover.

Thank you, dear God,
for the blessing of the old and the
    blessing of the new.

Lois Rock

Everyday Living

Day by day,
dear Lord, of thee
three things I pray:
to see thee more clearly,
love thee more dearly,
follow thee more nearly,
day by day.

Richard, bishop of Chichester
(1197–1253)

Dear Lord Jesus, we shall have this day only once; before it is gone, help us to do all the good we can, so that today is not a wasted day.

Stephen Grellet (1773–1855)

May I learn something new
every day.

May I do something new
every day.

May I learn something good
every day.

May I do something good
every day.

Bless to me, O Lord,
the work of my hands.
Bless to me, O God,
the work of my mind.
Bless to me, O God,
the work of my heart.

Author unknown

Holy Spirit of God,
be close to me
in the rushing wind,
and make me bold to do good.
Be close to me
in the golden fire
and help me to deeds
of shining goodness.

Father,
I am seeking:
I am hesitant and uncertain,
but will you, O God,
watch over each step of mine
and guide me.

St Augustine (354–430)

Teach us, Lord,
to serve you as you deserve,
to give and not to count the cost,
to fight and not to heed the wounds,
to toil and not to seek for rest,
to labour and not to seek for any reward
save that of knowing that we do your will.

St Ignatius Loyola (1491–1556)

May I be no one's enemy, and may I be the friend of that which lasts for ever.

May I never quarrel with those nearest: and if I do, may I be quick to restore the friendship.

May I love only what is good: always seek it and work to achieve it.

May I wish for everyone to find happiness and not envy anyone their good fortune.

May I never gloat when someone who has wronged me suffers ill fortune.

When I have done or said something wrong, may I not wait to be told off, but instead be angry with myself until I have put things right.

May I win no victory that harms either me or those who compete against me.

May I help those who have quarrelled to be friends with each other again.

May I, as far as I can, give practical help to my friends and anyone who is in need.

May I never fail a friend who is in danger.

When I visit those who are grieving may I find the right words to help heal their pain.

May I respect myself.

May I always control my emotions.

May I train myself to be gentle and not allow myself to become angry.

May I never whisper about wicked people and the things they have done, but rather seek to spend my time with good people and to follow their good example.

Eusebius (3rd century, adapted)

Lord, make us to walk in your way:
'Where there is love and wisdom, there is
  neither fear nor ignorance;
where there is patience and humility,
  there is neither anger nor annoyance;
where there is poverty and joy, there is
  neither greed nor avarice;
where there is peace and contemplation,
there is neither care nor restlessness;
where there is the fear of God to guard
  the dwelling, there no enemy can enter;
where there is mercy and prudence, there
  is neither excess not harshness';
this we know through your Son,
    Christ our Lord.

St Francis of Assisi (1181–1226)

Lord, make me an instrument of your peace.
Where there is hatred, let me sow love,
Where there is injury, pardon,
Where there is doubt, faith,
Where there is despair, hope,
Where there is darkness, light,
Where there is sadness, joy.

O Divine Master, grant that I may not so
much seek to be consoled as to console, not
so much to be understood as to understand,
not so much to be loved as to love; for it is
in giving that we receive, it is in pardoning
that we are pardoned, it is in dying that we
awake to eternal life.

A prayer associated with St Francis of Assisi

PRAYERS

FOR

Forgiveness

Father,
Forgive us the wrongs we have done,
As we forgive the wrongs that others
    have done to us.

From the prayer that Jesus taught (Matthew 6:11)

From the mud
a pure white flower

From the storm
a clear blue sky

As we pardon
one another

God forgives us
from on high.

Dear God,
For the silly things I have done wrong
I am sorry.

For the serious things I have done wrong
I am sorry.

For the things I didn't even know were
   wrong
I am sorry.

For all the things I need to put right
Make me strong.

Dear God,
When people shout in anger
help me to speak calmly;

When people threaten to hit me and
    hurt me
keep me from striking back;

When people try to lead me into a
    world of wrongdoing
give me the strength to walk away
    and a safe place to go:

A place of refuge,
a place of healing,
a place of forgiveness.

O Lord, remember not only the men and women of good will, but also those of ill will. But do not remember all the suffering they have inflicted on us; remember the fruits we have borne, thanks to this suffering – our comradeship, our loyalty, our courage, our generosity, the greatness of heart which has grown out of all this, and when they come to judgment let all the fruits which we have borne be their forgiveness.

Prayer written by an unknown prisoner in Ravensbruck concentration camp and left by the body of a dead child

Help

May God, the Lord, guide me to safety
May God's angels hide me from harm
May saints gather near me to quieten
   my fears
And all of my worries to calm.

Dear God,
I've been injured.
I've been wounded.
I've been hurt.
I've been damaged.

I want to be
mended,
patched,
fixed,
healed.

Lois Rock

Give us, O God, the needs the body feels,
Give us, God, the need-things of the soul;
Give us, O God, the balm which body
   heals,
Give us, God, the soul-balm which makes
   whole.

Poems of the Western Highlanders

Every day
in silence we remember

those whom we loved
to whom we have said a last goodbye.

Every day
in silence we remember.

Lois Rock

As the rain hides the stars, as the autumn mist hides the hills, as the clouds veil the blue of the sky, so the dark happenings of my lot hide the shining of thy face from me. Yet, if I may hold thy hand in the darkness, it is enough. Since I know that, though I may stumble in my going, thou dost not fall.

Author unknown

PRAYERS

FOR

People We Love

Father God,
Gather us all into a circle of friendship
and circle us about with your love.

Dear God,
Bless the generations:
the tiny babies,
fresh from heaven's sunrise;
the growing children,
exploring the bright new world;
the grown-ups,
travelling life's dusty road;
the older people,
enjoying the colours of the setting sun
where earth's horizon touches heaven.

Father of all mankind, make the roof of my house wide enough for all opinions, oil the door of my house so it opens easily to friend and stranger, and set such a table in my house that my whole family may speak kindly and freely around it. Amen.

Prayer from Hawaii

Father God,
Bless those who love us:

Those who make for us a safe home –
Bless them with your love.

Those who provide the things we need –
Bless them with your love.

Those who live too far away to visit –
Bless them with your love.

Those who remember us in their prayers –
Bless them with your love.

Dear God,
Guard our friendships:

Encourage us,
that we may encourage one another.

Inspire us,
that we may inspire one another.

Strengthen us,
that we may strengthen one another.

Remember us,
that we may remember one another.

God bless the house from roof to ground
With love encircle it around.
God bless each window, bless each door,
Be Thou our home for evermore.

Lois Rock

May the road rise up to meet you,
may the wind be always at your back,
may the sun shine upon your face,
the rains fall soft upon your fields
and, until we meet again,
may God hold you in the palm of
    his hand.

Author unknown

PRAYERS

FOR

A World in Need

The blessing of rain
The blessing of sun
To all the world
To everyone.

Lois Rock

May we learn from each other
how to give, how to receive;
how, in joy, to celebrate
and how, in pain, to grieve;
how to fight for what is right
yet not do any wrong;
how to be the family
to which we all belong.

There's trouble in the fields, Lord,
The crops are parched and dry.
We water them with tears, Lord,
So help us, hear our cry.

There's trouble in our hearts, Lord,
The world is full of pain.
Set us to work for healing,
Send blessings down like rain.

Lois Rock

Dear God,
We pray for those
who long to work
but can find no employment.

We pray for those
who work long hours
but are not paid a living wage.

We pray for those
whose tiny handful of wealth
will not pay the prices that are
demanded.

May those of us who have money
learn to be thrifty with ourselves
and both generous and just towards
others.

We pray, mighty God, for those who
    struggle
that their life's flickering flame may not
    be snuffed out.
We pray for the poor and deprived,
for those exploited by the powerful
    and greedy,
and for a more human sharing of the
    plenty
you have given your world.

Prayer from India

Love is giving, not taking,
mending, not breaking,
trusting, believing,
never deceiving,
patiently bearing
and faithfully sharing
each joy, every sorrow,
today and tomorrow.

Author unknown

Peaceable Jesus
You took the loaves and fishes
and fed a multitude.

I offer you this day
a tiny gift of squabbles I refused to fight.

Please will you multiply it
among the nations of the world
so that people will turn from war
and live in peace.

We pray for those
for whom today is like the windswept
    mountain:
give them comfort.

We pray for those
for whom today is like the stormy sea:
give them calm.

We pray for those
for whom today is like the darkest night:
give them hope.

Watch, dear Lord, with those who wake, or watch, or weep tonight, and give your angels charge over those who sleep;

Tend your sick ones, O Lord Christ, rest your weary ones, bless your dying ones, soothe your suffering ones, pity your afflicted ones, shield your joyous ones, and all for your love's sake. Amen.

St Augustine (354–430)

PRAYERS

FOR

Our Fragile World

God's own peace to the mountain,
God's own peace to the plain:
God's own Paradise garden
Grow in the world again.

Lois Rock

Father God,
Help us learn to live
in your wild and fragile world:

the trembling earth
the tumbling rivers
the tumultuous seas.

May your people all find
a harbour
a haven
a home.

Save me a clean stream, flowing
to unpolluted seas;

lend me the bare earth, growing
untamed flowers and trees.

May I share safe skies
when I wake, every day,

with birds and butterflies?
Grant me a space where I can play

with water, rocks, trees, and sand;
lend me forests, rivers, hills, and sea.

Keep me a place in this old land,
somewhere to grow, somewhere to be.

Jane Whittle

I think of the diverse majesty
Of all the creatures on the earth
Some with the power to terrify
And others that only bring mirth
I think of their shapes and their colours
Their secret and curious ways
And my heart seems to yearn for a
    language
That will sing their Great Maker's praise

Lois Rock

May we walk gently among the animals
Respecting their grazing
Respecting their hunting.

May we walk gently among the forests
Respecting their seasons
Of growing and falling.

May we walk gently beside the waters
Respecting their flooding
Their ebbing and flowing.

May we walk gently upon our planet
Its lands and its oceans
Their shifting and drifting.

O God, we thank you for this earth, our home; for the wide sky and the blessed sun, for the salt sea and the running water, for the everlasting hills and the never-resting winds, for the trees and the common grass underfoot.

We thank you for our senses by which we hear the songs of birds, and see the splendour of the summer fields, and taste of the autumn fruits, and rejoice in the feel of the snow, and smell the breath of the spring.

Grant us a heart wide open to all
this beauty; and save our souls
from being so blind that we pass
unseeing when even the common
thornbush is aflame with your
glory, O God our creator, who
lives and reigns for ever and ever.

Walter Rauschenbusch (1861–1918)

PRAYERS

OF

Blessing

May the grace of Christ our Saviour,
And the Father's boundless love,
With the Holy Spirit's favour,
Rest upon us from above.

John Newton (1725–1807)

Lord, keep us safe this night,
Secure from all our fears;
May angels guard us while we sleep,
Till morning light appears.

John Leland (1754–1841)

Who made the night-time shadows?
Who made the silver stars?
Who made the moon that floats on high
Where clouds and angels are?

The One who made the morning sun,
The daytime sky of blue,
The One who made both you and me
And loves both me and you.

Thou angel of God who hast charge of me
From the dear Father of mercifulness,
The shepherding kind of the fold of the
   saints
To make round about me this night;

Drive from me every temptation and
   danger,
Surround me on the sea of
   unrighteousness,
And in the narrows, crooks, and straits,
Keep thou my coracle, keep it always.

Be thou a bright flame before me,
Be thou a guiding star above me,
Be thou a smooth path below me,
And be a kindly shepherd behind me.
Today, tonight and for ever.

I am tired and I a stranger,
Lead thou me to the land of angels;
For me it is time to go home
To the court of Christ, to the peace
    of heaven.

Carmina Gadelica

Send your peace into my heart, O Lord,
that I may be contented
with your mercies of this day and
    confident
of your protection for this night;
and having forgiven others,
even as you forgive me,
may I go to my rest in peaceful trust
through Jesus Christ, our Lord, Amen.

St Francis of Assisi (1181–1226)

Peace of the running waves to you,
Deep peace of the flowing air to you,
Deep peace of the quiet earth to you,
Deep peace of the shining stars to you,
Deep peace of the shades of night to you,
Moon and stars always giving light to you,
Deep peace of Christ, the Son of Peace,
    to you.

Author unknown

Index of First Lines